Ephesians

BRINGING HEAVEN TO EARTH

Kevin Harney

ZondervanPublishingHouse

Grand Rapids, Michigan

A Division of HarperCollinsPublishers

Ephesians: Bringing Heaven to Earth
Copyright © 1995 by Kevin Harney

Requests for information should be addressed to:

🏭 ZondervanPublishingHouse
Grand Rapids, Michigan 49530

ISBN: 0–310–49841–4

Cover design by Jeff Sharpton, PAZ Design Group
Cover photograph © Larry Ulrich
Interior design by Joe Vriend

Printed in the United States of America

01 02 /❖ DP / 10 9 8 7 6 5

CONTENTS

GREAT BOOKS OF THE BIBLE

Every book of the Bible is important, because each one is inspired by God. But certain books draw us to them time and again for their strong encouragement, powerful teaching, and practical wisdom. The Great Books of the Bible Series brings into one collection eight biblical books that distinguish themselves either because of their undisputed excellence or because they are perennial favorites.

The Psalms, with their poetic imagery, help us express our emotions to God and see the myriad ways God works during the best and worst times of our lives. Two books—Proverbs in the Old Testament and James in the New Testament—offer practical wisdom for dealing with the decisions and realities of everyday life. The gospel of John gives us the most intimate and personal view of Jesus, the God-become-man who is Savior and Lord.

Three books are letters written by the apostle Paul. Romans is Paul's masterpiece—the clearest and fullest explanation of the gospel found in Scripture; there we see our world through God's eyes. Philippians shows us how to experience joy when we are under pressure. Ephesians explores the crucial role of the church as a living community, giving us just a little taste of heaven on earth as we seek to serve the Lord.

The series ends where the Bible does—with Revelation, where we glimpse our glorious future, when all things will become new.

Whether you are a new student of God's Word or one who has studied these books many times before, you will find here new insights and fresh perspectives that will make the Bible come alive for you.

The Great Books of the Bible Series is designed to be flexible. You can use the guides in any order. You can use them individually or in a small group or Sunday school class.

Leader's notes are provided in the back of each guide. They show how to lead a group discussion, provide additional information on questions, and suggest ways to deal with problems that may come up in the discussion. With such helps, someone with little or no experience can lead an effective study.

Suggestions for Individual Study

1. Begin each study with prayer. Ask God to help you understand the passage and to apply it to your life.

2. A good modern translation, such as the *New International Version,* the *New American Standard Bible,* or the *New Revised Standard Version,* will give you the most help. Questions in this guide are based on the *New International Version.*

3. Read and reread the passage(s). You must know what the passage says before you can understand what it means and how it applies to you.

4. Write your answers in the spaces provided in the study guide. This will help you to express clearly your understanding of the passage.

5. Keep a Bible dictionary handy. Use it to look up unfamiliar words, names, or places.

Suggestions for Group Study

1. Come to the study prepared. Careful preparation will greatly enrich your time in group discussion.

2. Be willing to join in the discussion. The leader of the group will not be lecturing, but will encourage people to discuss what they have learned in the passage. Plan to share what God has taught you in your individual study.

3. Stick to the passage being studied. Base your answers on the verses being discussed rather than on outside authorities such as commentaries or your favorite author or speaker.

4. Try to be sensitive to the other members of the group. Listen attentively when they speak, and be affirming whenever you can. This will encourage more hesitant members of the group to participate.

5. Be careful not to dominate the discussion. By all means participate! But allow others to have equal time.

6. If you are the discussion leader, you will find additional suggestions and helpful ideas in the leader's notes.

BRINGING HEAVEN TO EARTH

People discover the church in different ways. My wife, Sherry, can't remember a time when church activities were not a central part of her weekly schedule. From birth she was part of a loving Christian community. The congregation of a few hundred believers was a spiritual home, full of rich fellowship, all the time she was growing up. Sherry looks back on her upbringing in the church with fondness and a thankful heart.

My experience was *very* different. My first memory of the church goes back to kindergarten. I have vague recollections of sitting on a hard wooden bench and seeing a large crucifix on the wall. I remember wandering through unfamiliar halls and climbing up on a counter in search of punch and cookies. The whole counter began to fall backward, and I went with it. Scalding coffee burned my chest and neck, and an ambulance rushed me to the hospital.

My next memory dates to third grade, when our baby-sitter took me to church and Sunday school. I was a special guest, so I received ten dollars in "Sunday School Bucks." I spent my play money in the Sunday school store and went home feeling pretty good about church. The next week I was worth only five dollars, and while I gladly spent my play money at the Sunday school store, I did wonder what I would be worth next Sunday. Nothing! No more Sunday School Bucks. I stopped attending shortly after discovering my depreciating worth.

That was it until adolescence. My sister joined a church youth group, and after resisting her invitations for many months, I finally agreed to attend a special event one Wednesday evening. To my surprise, more than five hundred high school students were there. I began to attend regularly, and as I heard the gospel message week after week, I eventually accepted Christ as my Savior.

From that moment on, I began to discover the wonder and beauty of the church. When I outgrew the youth group, I had another experience of Christian community in a small group of eight young men who met for Bible study and prayer every Thursday morning before water polo practice. I went on to discover the church and community in a variety of settings.

After Sherry and I married, we began to experience the church together. We have worshiped in small congregations and large, in traditional sanctuaries and in warehouses. In each place we have been amazed by the presence of God's Holy Spirit and have tasted a little of what heaven must be like.

The church at its best gives us a foretaste of what lies ahead for us in eternity. The good thing is that here and now, by God's grace, we can have a little bit of heaven on earth.

About the Book of Ephesians

During his missionary service, the apostle Paul was repeatedly in trouble with either religious or civil authorites, and he often found himself in prison. When he was in chains, he kept in touch with the churches he had founded and visited through letters and personal couriers. He wrote his letter to the Ephesians while he was in prison, most likely in Rome. The city of Ephesus, in what is now the nation of Turkey, had a major harbor with access to the Aegean Sea and was located on a prominent trade route. At the time Paul founded its Christian community, the city was also a center of pagan worship.

This letter, often called the "Royal Epistle," stands out among all of Paul's letters as his definitive teaching on the church. Ephesians is a book about restoration and healing. In it Paul tells of God's plan to reconcile all things to himself, things in heaven and on earth. As we are restored in relationship to God, we are also reconciled to each other. And as God heals these relationships, he then binds us together into one glorious body, his church. In Ephesians we learn that the scope of God's work goes well beyond what we can see, touch, and experience with our senses. God's plan reaches to the highest heaven. Ephesians opens our eyes to the invisible heavenly realm of the spiritual world. As we find our places in his church, we are able to experience a foretaste of heaven on earth.

Study 1
The Blessings of God

Ephesians 1

I n my junior year of college a friend asked me if I would preach at a small church in Chicago. It was a house-church with about fifty people in attendance. I agreed to preach, and I began to prepare a message from the first chapter of Ephesians.

The unique part of this experience was that most of the fifty church members were just beginning to learn English. My friend's name was Demetrius, and he was born and raised in Thessalonica, Greece. Like him, most of the congregation spoke Greek fluently.

Demetrius interpreted as I preached. The congregation was warm and friendly and seemed to relate well with what I was saying. Their smiles and nodding heads affirmed that my message was hitting the mark. I spoke with enthusiasm, Demetrius interpreted with equal excitement, and the small congregation listened intently. Everything seemed to be going fine.

As I spoke about the church at Ephesus and gave the apostle Paul's greeting, I asked a simple question: "Whom is Paul talking about when he refers to 'the saints in Ephesus'?" I answered my own rhetorical question with the statement, "He is speaking of all the believers."

I explained that *all Christians are saints* in God's eyes. As I spoke these words and clarified Paul's view of sainthood, I realized very quickly that I was losing my audience. They might not have spoken much English, but the universal language of furrowed brows, confused expressions, and shaking heads spoke volumes. *They did not agree with me!*

After the message we had an open discussion (with interpretation), and several people explained their concern. Most of them came from a church background where a few select people are made "saints" by the church. They expressed their honest belief that they would never be able to attain this high and special status of sainthood.

1. What mental pictures come to mind when you hear the word *saint?*

   Perhaps you have known someone whom you would call a saint or regard as having lived a "saintly" life. What was it about his or her life that impressed you?

2. Read Ephesians 1:1–14. Would you expect someone to call you a saint? Why or why not?

3. Paul says we have been blessed in Christ "with every spiritual blessing" (v. 3). What are some of the spiritual blessings you have received through Jesus Christ?

4. In this passage we find a wonderful synopsis of the gospel. How would you define these three very important words (vv. 7–8)?

   — Redemption

   — Forgiveness

   — Grace

How do we experience God's redemption, forgiveness, and grace in our daily lives?

5. What concepts come to mind when you read the words "the riches of God's grace that he *lavished* on us" (vv. 7–8)?

   How have you experienced the working of God's grace and goodness in your life?

6. Why is the blood of Jesus a central element of the gospel message (v. 7)?

7. What is the place and work of the Holy Spirit in our salvation (vv. 13–14)?

   What is the work of the Holy Spirit in our continued spiritual growth?

8. Read Ephesians 1:15–23. What does Paul ask God to give the Christians at the church of Ephesus?

How can each of these qualities help believers grow in faith as God's saints?

9. Paul asks God to open the spiritual eyes of the Ephesians so that they may see three things. What is the significance of each (vv. 18–19)?

— To see the *hope* to which we have been called

— To see the *riches* of his glorious inheritance

— To see his *great power* for all who believe

10. Paul compares the power available to us with the same power with which Christ rose from the dead. What does it mean to walk in the "resurrection power" of Jesus?

How can we learn to do that (vv. 19–22)?

11. What do we learn about Jesus in verses 20–23?

How should the truth of these passages mold and shape the way we worship Jesus?

12. What does Paul mean when he calls the church "Christ's body"?

What are some meaningful parallels between the human body and the church as the body of Christ?

13. What can we do to strengthen and uphold the body of Christ?

Memory Verse I pray also that the eyes of your heart may be enlightened in order that you may know the hope to which he has called you, the riches of his glorious inheritance in the saints.

—Ephesians 1:18

Between Studies

Use Paul's prayer in Ephesians 1 as a guideline for the coming week.

Day 1: Thank God for making you a saint through the death and resurrection of Jesus (v. 15).

Day 2: Spend time thanking the Lord for your fellow saints in the faith (v. 16).

Day 3: Pray for God's wisdom to fill the life of a friend who needs direction from the Lord (v. 17).

Day 4: Ask God to open your eyes to see the hope and the rich inheritance that you have in Christ (v. 18).

Day 5: Ask God to show you how to have the resurrection power of Jesus in your daily life (vv. 19–20).

Day 6: Praise God for saving you through the shed blood of Jesus (vv. 20–22).

Day 7: Pray for strength and health in the body of Christ, the church (vv. 22–23).

Our Unity in Christ

Ephesians 2

Imagine that you are driving along the interstate highway in the open country. There is little traffic, the sun is shining, and your eyes are taking in the beauty of the countryside around you. Your mind is at ease, and you are enjoying the quiet solitude of your drive.

All of a sudden your whole body tenses, and your heart begins to race. You hear the faint sound of a police siren behind you. As your eyes dart to the rearview mirror, your fears are realized when you see the flashing red light on top of the car in the distance. Your eyes immediately jump from the mirror to the speedometer: 78 miles per hour!

How did that happen? The last time you looked at the speedometer you were only doing 60. You had no intention of speeding, but here you are, slowing down and pulling over with a police officer rolling to a stop behind you. As the officer gets out of his car and walks to yours, your mind races to decide what to say.

Many of us have found ourselves in this or a similar situation. Few of us would greet the officer with a cheerful, "Good afternoon, officer, I was going seventy-eight in a sixty-five zone, and I demand that you give me the full fine for my crime!" If we are honest with ourselves and others, the last thing we want at this point is justice. What we want is grace!

1. What do you think you would say to the officer if you were pulled over in this situation?

How do you define *justice,* and how do you define *grace?*

2. Read Ephesians 2:1–10. What does Paul mean when he says, "You were dead in your transgressions and sins" (v. 1)? That is, what is spiritual death?

3. What are some of the enticements and lures of Satan that Christians face today (vv. 2–3)?

4. God's life-giving plan was motivated by his great love for us. How have you experienced God's great love and mercy recently in your life (v. 4)?

5. What does it mean to be "alive with Christ" (v. 5)?

   How does this "new life" affect your understanding of this life and eternity?

6. How does Paul contrast the understanding of salvation by grace and the mistaken understanding of salvation by good works (vv. 5–9)?

What are some of the possible consequences when a person or a church believes salvation comes by good works rather than by grace?

7. Although we are not saved *by* good works, we are saved *to do* good works (v. 10). What is the difference between the two concepts?

What are some of the good works God has called us to do?

8. Paul reminds the Ephesian believers of the status they had *outside* of Jesus, before they came to know him. What is the significance of each phrase (vv. 11–13)?

— "Separate from Christ"

— "Excluded from citizenship in Israel"

— "Foreigners to the covenants of the promise"

— "Without hope"

— "Without God in the world"

9. Paul speaks of the barriers between Jews and Gentiles coming down because of Christ's work (vv. 14–18). What are the practical and spiritual results?

How does faith in Jesus remove our prejudice and judgment of those who are different from us?

10. Paul talks about what we *are* and what we *are not*. What is the meaning of each statement (vv. 19–20)?

— You are *no longer* foreigners and aliens

— You *are* fellow citizens

— You *are* members of God's household

11. What is the function of a cornerstone in a building, and how does Christ serve this same function in his church (vv. 20–22)?

How does Jesus join believers together into one body or temple?

Memory Verse For it is by grace you have been saved, through faith—and this not from yourselves, it is the gift of God—not by works, so that no one can boast.

—Ephesians 2:8–9

Between Studies

Take time to reflect on the wonder of God's great grace. Here are three exercises to help you do so.

1. Sing and meditate on the words of some great hymns that celebrate the grace of God. Most hymn and chorus books have a topical

index. Use this to find three or four songs to help you express praise for the rich gift of grace.

2. Use a Bible concordance to look up ten or so passages about God's grace. Study these passages and reflect on what God has done to extend his amazing grace to you.

3. List on paper all the things you have that are a gift from the gracious hand of God. Think about spiritual blessings, people whom the Lord has placed in your life, material things the Lord has given you, opportunities God has brought your way, and anything else that comes to mind. Let this list become a tool for praising the Lord for all his gifts of grace.

12/5
growth of our church
Nancy getting a job
Dan's brother wedding

STUDY 3

GOD'S MYSTERY

EPHESIANS 3

From my childhood I have loved a good mystery. I can remember reading "Five-Minute Mystery" books and trying to figure out "who dun it." I remember watching Ellery Queen mysteries on television and doing my best to solve the case before the sleuth figured it out. And then there's Columbo—the sense of anticipation we feel as he methodically unravels the complex web of relationships, clues, and evidence to close in on the suspect. From Sherlock Holmes to Agatha Christie to the board game *Clue,* most of us love a good mystery.

What is it about the human spirit that yearns to explain a complicated mystery? Why do we find so much satisfaction and joy when we finally solve a puzzle?

1. Why do you think mysteries fascinate us?

2. Read Ephesians 3:1–13. The word *mystery* is used four times in this brief passage. What is the mystery Paul is writing about?

    3, 4, 6, 9

19

How did God reveal this great mystery to humanity?

How does the truth of this mystery still affect the world today?

3. What would Gentiles, not having grown up in the Jewish faith, take each of the following statements to mean (v. 6)?

— You are "heirs together with Israel"

— You have become "members together of one body"

— You are "sharers together in the promise in Christ Jesus"

4. Why did Paul see himself as "less than the least of all God's people" (v. 8)?

What does God's using a man with Paul's background for such a great task suggest about our usefulness to God?

5. Paul said that through Christ we can approach God "with freedom and confidence" (v. 12). What does it mean to approach God with freedom?

What does it mean to approach him with confidence?

6. Read Ephesians 3:14–21. In your own words, what does Paul pray for in the Ephesians' behalf?

    What can we learn from Paul's example as we pray for ourselves and others?

7. What does it mean to be "rooted and established in love" (v. 17)?

8. Paul speaks of Christ's love as being wide, long, high, and deep. How has God revealed the great depth of his love for humanity (v. 18)?

    How have you experienced the greatness of God's love in your life?

9. Read the benediction—the blessing—in Ephesians 3:20–21 aloud. These verses state in expressive language that God can do things beyond what we expect or dream. How have

you experienced the truth of this passage in your family, your church, or some other situation?

Memory Verse Now to him who is able to do immeasurably more than all we ask or imagine, according to his power that is at work within us.

—Ephesians 3:20

Between Studies

Take time to meditate on the truth of Ephesians 3:20–21. God can—and does—grant blessings far beyond what we ask or even dream. Reflect on your past and remember the great blessings God has given you. It might be helpful to divide your life into time periods (childhood, junior high school, senior high, young adulthood, and so on) and write down some of the ways God has worked in your life.

DISCOVERING MY PLACE IN CHRIST'S BODY

EPHESIANS 4

As we got ready to pull out of the grocery store parking lot we saw a sight filled with power and beauty. Both my wife and I sat in stunned amazement and wonder. After we saw it, we were both silent for a time and simply sat in quiet reflection.

What did we see that had such an impact on us? A sunset? A rainbow after a spring shower? No, it was none of the glories of the natural world. What we saw might not at first glance have seemed memorable, but it was to us.

We saw a quadriplegic and a blind man out for an afternoon walk.

The man in the wheelchair, having no use of his limbs, gave verbal directions to his friend as they moved along: He lent his ability to see. The blind man used the strength of his legs and directed the chair: He offered his physical strength. Together they made fairly good time and seemed to be enjoying their walk together.

Neither could have taken the walk alone. Either of these men could have chosen to stay inside that day. Together they found a wholeness and strength they did not possess on their own.

For my wife and me, this experience became a parable of spiritual living, a powerful illustration of the body of Christ, the church. As believers we all have weaknesses and strengths. When we walk together, letting our unique gifts be used by the Lord, we are all made stronger. We all have something to offer to his service.

1. Describe an occasion when you saw people working together in a way that made them stronger and more effective than they would have been if they had been working alone.

    Describe an occasion when someone came alongside you and offered help and strength when you were in need.

2. Read Ephesians 4:1–16. What four exhortations does Paul give believers in this passage (v. 2)?

    What are some specific ways we can follow these exhortations today?

    Exhortation   **Manifestation**

    humble
    patient
    gentle
    bearing c one another

3. Paul lists seven points of Christian oneness (vv. 4–6). Consider why each is important for Christian unity:

    — One body — church
    — One Spirit — believe in same thing
    — One hope — eternal life
    — One lord — Jesus
    — One faith — commitment to Christ
    — One baptism — sign of entry into church
    — One God — faith

4. List the spiritual gifts Paul mentions and define them. What is the function of each gift among God's people (v. 11)?

Gift	Definition	Function
apostles		establishing church
prophets		made known message
evangelists		spread word
pastors & teachers		

5. Paul cites some wonderful things that result in the body of Christ when spiritual gifts are used correctly. Which of these results do you see in your church (vv. 12–16)?

6. What are some false teachings that can enter the church and spread damage and dissension among God's people (v. 14)?

What can we do to prevent false teaching from entering the church?

7. What does it mean to speak the truth in love (v. 15)?

How can speaking the truth in love be difficult?

Why is it important to do this even when it might be hard?

8. Read Ephesians 4:17–32. What does Paul mean when he says to "put off the old self" and "put on the new self"?

9. If we liken the old self to clothing, what are the "old garments" Christians need to take off (vv. 25–31)?

How do we discard the "rags" of our old life and don the garments of our new life in Christ?

What can happen if we continue to wear the tattered garments?

10. Paul calls Christians to put on the new "clothing" of faith in Jesus. Why is each important for our continued spiritual growth?

— Truthful speech (v. 25)

— Appropriate anger (v. 26)

— Honest work (v. 28)

— Edifying speech (v. 29)

— Kindness (v. 32)

— Compassion (v. 32)

— Forgiveness (v. 32)

Memory Verse There is one body and one Spirit—just as you were called to one hope when you were called—one Lord, one faith, one baptism; one God and Father of all, who is over all and through all and in all.

—Ephesians 4:4–6

Between Studies

Use the lists above from questions 9 and 10 as a starting point for reflection and prayer. Identify one piece of "spiritual clothing" that you are still wearing from the old life. Take time to pray for the strength to strip it off and leave it in the past. You may want to have a close Christian friend pray for you and keep you accountable in this.

Also, choose one of the pieces of "spiritual clothing" we are called to put on as we grow in our new life in Christ. Pray for the strength to grow in this regard.

DISCOVERING MY PLACE IN THE FAMILY OF GOD

EPHESIANS 5:1 – 6:9

For almost a decade Americans tuned their television sets to watch a situation comedy that seemingly struck a nerve in the public consciousness. The location was not spectacular—a bar in Boston named Cheers. The characters were a ragtag bunch of misfits: a bartender who was a recovering alcoholic, a know-it-all mailman, a cynical, sharp-tongued waitress, an unemployed accountant who never spent time with his wife, a naive country boy, and a psychologist who needed counseling as badly as most of his patients. This bunch hardly has the feel of a national phenomenon.

Why did this show have so much appeal? The answer may be found in the theme song. The message of the song is simple yet profound: "You want to go where you can see our troubles are all the same. You want to go where everybody knows your name."

We all want to belong. Each of us has a hunger to find a place where we can walk in the door and everyone will shout our name in a warm welcome. There is a basic human need to have a place where we are recognized, accepted, and loved.

1. In what places and situations do you see people looking for a sense of belonging?

How can a strong church meet this need?

How can loving homes meet this need?

2. Read Ephesians 5:1–7. In the household of faith, God is our Father, and as his children we are called to imitate him. In what specific ways can we follow the example of the Lord (v. 1)?

3. What do you think Paul has in mind when he describes the sacrifice of Jesus—the brutal act of crucifixion—as a "fragrant offering" to God (v. 2)?

4. Paul lists some qualities that should *not* be part of our lives, ranging from sexual immorality to coarse joking. Why are we commanded to stay away from these practices (vv. 3–7)? That is, what are their potential consequences for us as members of the household of faith?

5. Paul says thankfulness should fill our lives and replace our sinful behavior. How do we develop a thankful heart (v. 4)?

6. Read Ephesians 5:8–20. Christians are "children of light." Paul lists the fruit of those who walk in the light. What is the importance of the following actions?

— Walking in goodness

— Growing in righteousness

— Exposing "fruitless deeds of darkness"

— Remaining silent about the things the disobedient do in the darkness

— "Making the most of every opportunity"

— Growing in understanding God's will

— Being "filled with the Spirit"

— Speaking to each other in "psalms, hymns, and spiritual songs"

— Singing and making music to the Lord in our hearts

— Always giving thanks to the Father

7. Read Ephesians 5:22–33. What counsel does Paul give to wives, and how should it be practiced in marriage today (vv. 22–24)?

8. What words of exhortation are given for husbands, and how should they be practiced in marriages today (vv. 25–33)?

9. Read Ephesians 6:1–4. What does it mean for children to obey their parents "in the Lord"?

How can children—younger and older—show honor?

10. What are the responsibilities of parents toward their children, and how can they fulfill these (v. 4)?

11. What can we do individually to build strong Christian homes where Christ is honored and faith is learned?

What can we do corporately?

Memory Verse Be imitators of God, therefore, as dearly loved children and live a life of love, just as Christ loved us and gave himself up for us as a fragrant offering and sacrifice to God.

—Ephesians 5:1–2

Between Studies

Take time to write a thank-you letter. Write to a person in your church family who has been an encouragement to you and has helped you grow in faith. Also, write a thank-you note to someone in your family who has helped you recently.

Study 6
Strength for the Battle

Ephesians 6:10-24

Beware of dog!

The warning was posted for everyone to see, in letters painted bright red. The sound of barking dogs behind the fence also acted as a caution to any trespassers. Who would be foolish enough to ignore the clearly posted warning?

THIN ICE! STAY OFF THE POND!

All you had to do was look at the pond and you could see the ice was not thick enough to hold a great deal of weight. The sign was a reminder of a potential threat to life. No one would be so bold as to walk on thin ice and risk her life—or would she?

PUT ON YOUR ARMOR! YOU ARE IN A BATTLE!

The devil is alive and well. He desires to destroy our lives, families, churches, and everything else we hold dear. Scripture gives the warning again and again, like a sign posted in the road: DANGER AHEAD! CAUTION! The Bible gives us ample warning about the reality, power, and work of the devil. We would never take these warnings lightly—or would we?

1. Besides those suggested above, what are some warnings people often ignore?

Why do you think people ignore warnings even when there is potential danger?

2. Read Ephesians 6:10–24. What is our source of strength for the spiritual battles we face?

What are some possible consequences if we try to stand in our own strength?

3. We are called to "stand against the devil's schemes." What are some of the schemes and tactics of the devil?

4. What are some of the names given for the devil in the Bible, and what does each one teach us about this enemy of our souls?

5. Paul uses the imagery of a Roman soldier's armor to describe our defenses against the devil. How does each part of the spiritual armor act as a defensive measure in our lives (vv. 14–17)?

— Truth

—Righteousness — *protects our heart*

—Peace — *shoes*

— Faith - *shield*

— Salvation - *helmet*

6. A strong defense is only half the battle. We also need to have a powerful weapon for an offensive attack. Why is the Word of God (the Bible) listed as the first weapon of attack in our spiritual battles (v. 17)?

7. Why is regular, disciplined study of the Word critical for believers who want to win the spiritual battles they face?

    What are possible consequences for those who neglect learning to use "the sword of the Spirit"?

8. Paul also reminds us of another mighty weapon in the spiritual battle. We are exhorted to use the weapon of prayer (v. 18). How can prayer be an effective weapon in our battle against the devil?

9. How have you seen God answer prayer in ways that broke the power and work of the devil?

10. What specific spiritual battles are being fought in your personal life, your community, or your church? What specific tactics can you use in this warfare?

11. Paul closes this letter with a simple request: "Pray also for me . . . so that I will fearlessly make known the mystery of the gospel." What can bring fear to our hearts and keep us from sharing the gospel?

How can we overcome these fears and share the gospel with confidence?

Memory Verse Finally, be strong in the Lord and in his mighty power. Put on the full armor of God so that you can take your stand against the devil's schemes.

—Ephesians 6:10–11

Between Studies

Begin each morning in the next week by meditating on Ephesians 6:10–18. Read this passage slowly and prayerfully. As you think about each piece of armor, ask the Lord to help you wear it no matter what you face during the day. The following is a suggested prayer.

Lord, let me wear truth like a belt firmly secured around my waist,
help me wear righteousness as a protecting breastplate,
teach me to wear a peace that will give secure footing wherever I
   might walk this day,

may I hold faith like a shield to defend me from the attack of the
devil,
and let the security of my salvation be a helmet of confidence
around my thinking.

After you have prayed for God to dress you in his armor, ask him
to help you take up the weapons you will need to fight against the
devil and his schemes.

Lord of victory and strength, help me to take up the sword of the
Spirit, which is your Word.
May your Word be in my heart and on my lips at all times.
Help me also to be a person of prayer, seeking your strength and
will in all things.
Give me confidence through your Word and strength through
prayer
so I may resist the devil and fight against his work in the world,
your church, and my life.

LEADER'S NOTES

Leading a Bible discussion—especially for the first time—can make you feel both nervous and excited. If you are nervous, realize that you are in good company. Many biblical leaders, such as Moses, Joshua, and the apostle Paul, felt nervous and inadequate to lead others (see, for example, 1 Corinthians 2:3). Yet God's grace was sufficient for them, just as it will be for you.

Some excitement is also natural. Your leadership is a gift to the others in the group. Keep in mind, however, that other group members also share responsibility for the group. Your role is simply to stimulate discussion by asking questions and encouraging people to respond. The suggestions listed below can help you to be an effective leader.

Preparing to Lead

1. Ask God to help you understand and apply the passage to your own life. Unless that happens, you will not be prepared to lead others.

2. Carefully work through each question in the study guide. Meditate and reflect on the passage as you formulate your answers.

3. Familiarize yourself with the leader's notes for the study. These will help you understand the purpose of the study and will provide valuable information about the questions in the study.

4. Pray for the various members of the group. Ask God to use these studies to make you better disciples of Jesus Christ.

5. Before the first meeting, make sure each person has a study guide. Encourage them to prepare beforehand for each study.

Leading the Study

1. Begin the study on time. If people realize that the study begins on schedule, they will work harder to arrive on time.

2. At the beginning of your first time together, explain that these studies are designed to be discussions, not lectures. Encourage everyone to participate, but realize that some may be hesitant

to speak during the first few sessions.

3. Read the introductory paragraph at the beginning of the discussion. This will orient the group to the passage being studied.

4. Read the passage aloud. You may choose to do this yourself, or you might ask for volunteers.

5. The questions in the guide are designed to be used just as they are written. If you wish, you may simply read each one aloud to the group. Or you may prefer to express them in your own words. Unnecessary rewording of the questions, however, is not recommended.

6. Don't be afraid of silence. People in the group may need time to think before responding.

7. Avoid answering your own questions. If necessary, rephrase a question until it is clearly understood. Even an eager group will quickly become passive and silent if they think the leader will do most of the talking.

8. Encourage more than one answer to each question. Ask, "What do the rest of you think?" or "Anyone else?" until several people have had a chance to respond.

9. Try to be affirming whenever possible. Let people know you appreciate their insights into the passage.

10. Never reject an answer. If it is clearly wrong, ask, "Which verse led you to that conclusion?" Or let the group handle the problem by asking them what they think about the question.

11. Avoid going off on tangents. If people wander off course, gently bring them back to the passage being considered.

12. Conclude your time together with conversational prayer. Ask God to help you apply those things that you learned in the study.

13. End on time. This will be easier if you control the pace of the discussion by not spending too much time on some questions or too little on others.

Study One	*The Blessings of God*
	Ephesians 1

Purpose   To reflect on the great blessings we receive when we are in Christ and to grow in our understanding of the church as a body of people bound together through the love and grace of Jesus.

Question 2   Once, while teaching an adult Sunday school class of about eighty people, all Christians, I asked those who believed they were saints to raise their hands. Only eight or nine people did so, sheepishly. I then said, "Raise your hand if you are a Christian," and all hands went up. We then discussed the truth that *every Christian is a saint*.

Although we may not feel very saintly much of the time, we need to remember that our status as saints comes from the finished work of Jesus on the cross, not from the righteousness of our lives. All Christians are saints in God's sight.

Question 4   Don't try to force these rich and meaningful words into rigid and sterile definitions. Most definitions offered will be a combination of devotional and theological understandings of these terms. Here are brief definitions for each word:

Redemption: To pay a price to buy something back. Jesus has paid the price for our sins through his death on the cross. When we accept Jesus and the price he has paid, we are redeemed and the penalty of our sins is paid in full.

Forgiveness: To treat someone who has wronged us as if he or she had not. Forgiveness does not require forgetting what happened (usually this is impossible); however, it does mean loving and treating the one who has wronged us as if he or she had done nothing wrong. Through Christ our sins are forgiven and God regards us as though we had never sinned. We are blameless in his sight.

Grace: Grace is the abundant and overflowing goodness of God that is poured out on us through the love of Jesus.

Grace has been defined with this simple acronym:

God's **R**iches **A**t **C**hrist's **E**xpense

Question 6   The New Testament is filled with reminders of the central importance of the blood of Jesus for the forgiveness of sins. It is through the sacrificial death of Jesus that the price for our sins and wrongs was paid. Some helpful passages for further study are Romans 3:21–26; 5:9–11; Colossians 1:15–20; Hebrews 9:11–22.

Question 7   This passage tells us that the Holy Spirit marks and seals us as a guarantee of our salvation. The Holy Spirit resides in the heart and life of every believer. The presence of the Spirit ensures our place in God's kingdom and reminds us that we belong to the Savior. A number of New Testament passages teach us about the presence and work of the Holy Spirit. For teaching on spiritual fruit, study Galatians 5:22–25. For teaching on spiritual gifts, study Romans 12:3–16 and 1 Corinthians 12–13.

Question 9   It is important to realize that all these blessings belong to all those who believe in Jesus. Paul's prayer is not for God to impart hope, spiritual riches, and power, but for believers to see what they *already have available*. Take time to discuss the great meaning and value of these possessions.

Question 10   The resurrection of Jesus is our source of power for daily living. We are lifted with Christ into the heavenly realms, and his resurrection power is "unleashed" in our lives. We may not feel the profound impact of this power at 9 o'clock Monday morning as the new week begins, but it is available.

Paul holds the resurrection of Christ as a central part of our faith. In the resurrection we discover not only the assurance of eternal life, but also power and strength to live for the Lord today. Take time to read Romans 6:1–14 and 1 Corinthians 15:12–57.

Question 12   Although Paul uses numerous illustrations to teach about the church, the imagery of the body of Christ is the most developed in his letters. The parallels between a physical body and the spiritual body of Christ are numerous. Explore them to the full. It might help to read part of Paul's teaching on the body of Christ in 1 Corinthians 12:12–26.

Study Two	*Our Unity in Christ*
	Ephesians 2

Purpose   To grow in our understanding of God's grace for all who believe and to see the transformation that comes in our lives when we truly live in the grace of Jesus.

Questions 2 and 5 Paul uses the terms *alive* and *dead* when refer-
ring to people who are inside and outside of Christ. These are clearly
being used to express the spiritual condition of the person.

Those who are in Christ and know his grace are "alive." They
have received the new birth Jesus told Nicodemus about in John 3.
All who call on Jesus as Savior know a new spiritual life that begins
at the point of faith and continues for eternity. This new life sets
believers free from the power and condemnation of sin. To be alive
in Jesus gives us new life, hope, and joy today as well as the assurance of spending eternity with the Lord.

Those who are are "dead in transgressions and sin" do not have
the power to resist temptation. They lack the hope and peace that
are found in Jesus alone. This life is experienced in a state of spiritual emptiness that affects every aspect of this life and will have
eternal consequences for all who reject Christ.

Question 6 Paul is careful to help us understand that our salvation is not a result of our good works or self-righteousness. Because
we are saved by grace, there is no room for boasting or self-exalta-
tion, only for humble thankfulness. Paul rejects any sense of gaining
salvation by our own good deeds.

Be aware that many Christians struggle with the false assump-
tion that personal works are a factor in receiving salvation. Even
though they may understand salvation to be a work of God, many
people still have a sense that they have to "measure up." Yet the reason Jesus came is that we can never be good enough to deserve God's
grace; salvation is *entirely* God's work. This assurance is essential to
of understanding the immeasurable depth of God's grace.

Questions 8 and 10 The most difficult statements to understand
are those that refer to *Israel* and *foreigners*. These have reference to
the Old Testament history of Israel. Israel was called out from
among the people of the earth to be God's chosen people. They
became a vehicle for God to pour out his blessing on the whole
earth (Genesis 12:1–3). God established covenants (agreements)
with Israel. Over the centuries, the people of Israel came to believe
that these promises, covenants, and blessings were reserved for
them alone.

In the days of Jesus and Paul, the Jews and the Gentiles (all non-
Jews) remained very separate—religiously, culturally, and socially.

41

Through Christ and the preaching of Paul, a new message was preached that declared Jews and Gentiles one in Christ—that is, whoever has faith in Christ has equal access to salvation by grace and equal standing before God, regardless of their religious history.

Question 9   The temple in Jerusalem had a dividing wall that kept all Gentiles from coming too close. This physical wall stood as a constant reminder that Jews and Gentiles were separate peoples. Through Christ the wall has been torn down and the two have become one. Paul is emphatic about the unity all Christians have by reason of the work of Jesus. This truth has deep implications on prejudice, racism, and any action or attitude motivated by prejudice.

You might want to discuss ways in which prejudice can subtly intrude in our own lives and in churches. Consider ways that we can recognize racial prejudice in ourselves and how we can resist it for the sake of Christ's reputation and the unity of the church.

Question 11   The cornerstone is the standard by which all the other stones in the building are measured. If the cornerstone is true, then all the measurements will be sound. With Christ as our cornerstone, we are bound together as living stones into one holy temple. When we are built together into the church with Jesus as the cornerstone, we will have unity and strength.

Study Three	*God's Mystery*
	Ephesians 3

Purpose   To grow in our understanding of the mystery of God's good news and to praise God for all his blessings.

Question 2   The mystery Paul speaks of is both simple and profound. Paul has alluded to the mystery in chapter 2, where he states that through the gospel of Christ all people are invited to share in the blessings God had earlier revealed to the Jewish nation. God's love, grace, and friendship are not reserved for a select few. Through the work of Jesus, the door is open to all who will believe by faith and receive the gift of grace. (See Colossians 1:24–27.)

This mystery continues to transform lives, churches, communities, and even nations. This is the truth that has changed the course of history. Whatever our culture or way of life, this mystery gives us access to the gift of God.

Question 3 These three statements reveal the complete inclusion of Gentiles in the faith. Although the first people to acknowledge Jesus as the Messiah were Jews, Paul was careful to let everyone know that Jesus had come to save all who would believe, Gentile or Jew. The Gentiles who were coming to faith in Jesus were to receive the full inheritance of God as heirs together with the people of Israel. They were also embraced in full fellowship as members of God's body, the church. Finally, the promises God had made to the people of Israel through the history of the Old Testament were available to Gentile converts as well.

Question 4 Although Paul knew that the Lord had revealed the mystery of the ages through him, he also had a humble realization of his own place and status. On various occasions Paul commented on his view of himself in relationship to his past and his calling. For further reflection, study Acts 7:54–8:3 and 1 Corinthians 15:9–11.

Question 7 Paul uses language from agriculture as an image of our intimacy with Jesus. Use this image and discuss the importance of deep roots for the health of a plant. Notice the parallels between deep roots for the life of a plant and the need for deep roots in God's love for us to grow in our faith.

Question 9 A time of thanksgiving and praise is appropriate for the close of this study.

| Study Four | *Discovering My Place in Christ's Body* Ephesians 4 |

Purpose To discover the unity and community we all have as members of Christ's body, the church.

Question 2 As we learn to live together in Christian community, we need to follow the teaching of Scripture. Only then can we hope to build strong churches, homes, and relationships. Paul lays down four guidelines for healthy and unified churches: humility, gentleness, patience, and love. If we cultivate these four qualities diligently, we will discover the unity of the Spirit and the bond of peace of which Paul speaks.

Question 3 The call to unity for God's people is not a call to uniformity or strict conformity. Although we all worship the same Lord and are led by the same Spirit, we do not all express our faith in the same way. There is great room for diversity in style of worship, architecture, liturgy, music, and other expressions of our Christian faith. We need to seek unity, but must not demand uniformity.

With this in mind we can look at Paul's seven points of oneness as the fundamental pillars of our faith on which to strive for unity. Despite our diversity of expression (see question 2), it is important in our day to seek Christian fellowship and offer support to others who love the Lord but may not be part of our church or denomination. We are called to walk in unity with all who serve Christ.

Question 4   Some helpful passages relating to the spiritual gifts that Paul mentions: apostles (Acts 1:21–22), prophets (1 Corinthians 14:3–4), evangelists (Acts 21:8; 1 Corinthains 1:17).

Question 6   We are called to hold fast to the truth God has revealed in his Word. False teaching must be opposed in the church even if it has the appearance of spirituality. In his letters Paul repeatedly warns against false teachers, who can prove disruptive to the unity and purity of the church.

False teaching can consist of worldly values as well as unbiblical doctrine. One example is the "health and wealth" gospel that promises instant prosperity for all who are in the faith.

Another is end-times preaching and date-setting that go beyond or conflict with the clear injunctions of Scripture. Last, there is rigid legalism that binds and burdens believers in contrast to the freedom promised in Christ.

Questions 8 to 10   Clothing offers a striking image for new life in Jesus. We must strip off the old, tattered rags of our previous life and be dressed in the new linens of life in Christ.

Try to be specific about how we can do away with the old and put on the new. While these matters may be too personal to discuss with others, working on these lists will help people come to grips with specific issues, both negatively (the ones they need to discard) and positively (the ones they need to cultivate).

Discovering My Place in the Family of God
Ephesians 5:1–6:9

Purpose To grow in our understanding of the church as a community of faith and to learn how we can strengthen our homes as a place where Christ is glorified and faith is learned.

Question 3 Paul's language comes from the Old Testament. The terms *fragrant* and *pleasing aroma* are used altogether more than forty times in the five books of Moses in reference to the Hebrews' sacrificial system. They imply that the sacrifices thus offered were well-pleasing to God and accepted as a means of reconciliation with him. Jesus' death as the perfect, once-for-all sacrifice (Hebrews 9:11–28) is declared pleasing to God and sufficient for reconciliation between us and God.

Question 4 Discussion should focus on why the sins Paul lists are harmful to Christians both individually and as members of the church. Because some of the behaviors—such as sexual immorality—seem more serious, with more obvious consequences than others, we do well to observe the ways in which each of these can be harmful to the body of Christ and our spiritual well-being. Consider a prayer time for people in the study who are struggling with one or another of these practices.

Question 6 Paul lists ten specific ways we can walk in the light of God. Take time to reflect on these exhortations and what we can do to nurture these practices in our churches, homes, and relationships. Note that unless the "children of light" demonstrate that spiritual illumination, the world will remain in darkness with no means to see the Father of light (see James 1:17).

Question 7 The rule for harmony in Christian relationships is *mutual submission* (v. 21). The marital relationship is based on genuine love for God and each other, expressed in humble fellowship. This forbids selfish exploitation by husbands.

Question 8 In the same way that Christ loves the church, husbands are to act on the basis of self-sacrifice, humble service, and unwavering love. If husbands diligently seek to love their wives with this kind of committed passion, mutual submission will grow naturally in their relationship.

45

Question 9   Paul reminds us of the fifth commandment (Exodus 20:12). Children are called to give honor and respect to their parents. This holds true for young children and adult children.

One important phrase here often gets overlooked: "in the Lord." For children to "obey their parents *in the Lord*" marks a dividing line between obedience and allegiance. If a parent's request is consistent with God's truth, children should obey. However, if a parent does not follow the Lord and calls a child to do something that is immoral in God's sight, children are not compelled to obey.

Question 10   The point is that parental authority is not authoritarian. Parenthood is not a billy club.

Study Six	*Strength for the Battle*
	Ephesians 6:10–24

Purpose   To help us identify the defensive and offensive tools God has given us to fight against the schemes of the devil.

Question 1   Many of us can tell stories of people who have ignored warnings and paid the price. From speed limits to the warnings of the surgeon general, we seem to play on the edge of warnings and try to get away with as much as we can. Some people may be willing to relate an experience of a warning ignored.

Question 4   Take time to consider some names given to the devil, because each one gives some insight into his tactics and works. Here are some to get you started: the father of lies (John 8:44), a roaring lion (1 Peter 5:8), the tempter (Matthew 4:3), and an angel of light (2 Corinthians 11:14).

Question 5   Each article in the armor protects in a particular way against a certain battle tactic. The metaphor of the battle armor is one of the most elaborate in the Bible and lends itself to helpful discussion about the Christian life.

Questions 6 and 7   Paul cites the Bible ("the sword of the Spirit") as the primary offensive weapon against the work of the devil. A striking biblical example of this truth is found in Matthew 4:1–11 and Luke 4:1–13, two accounts of Jesus' temptation in the wilderness. The primary weapon Jesus used against the enemy when he was tempted was the Word of God. Take the time to read one of these accounts.

Questions 8 and 9 It has been said, "Prayer is not preparation for the battle, it is the battle." We need to learn how to pray for God's strength for ourselves and for other believers. We also need to identify where the enemy is working and pray against his schemes and tactics. When we continue faithfully in prayer, God hears our prayers and they do make a difference. There is more power in the name of Jesus than most of us ever realize or dream.

Question 11 Many Christians feel great apprehension—and even fear—about sharing their faith. Fear of rejection, fear of offending someone, and appearing to be a religious fanatic are some of the common reasons for this reluctance to witness. Many Christians love the Lord and long to share their faith but are fearful of the possible consequences.

Allow people to express their fears honestly. Others may want to describe ways they have been able to share their faith, but they must be cautioned to express this success lovingly without displaying an attitude of superiority. Emphasize that there is not one specific way we must share the gospel, but that we all are to let our light shine. Often a simple testimony about the difference our faith makes in our daily life can be a great starting point. A testimony of a changed life presents the gospel in a way almost anyone can understand.